Where Your House
Is Now

Where Your House
Is Now

prose poems

LOUIS JENKINS

NODIN PRESS

Cover painting "Looking for Daphne" by Frank Sampson courtesy of the artist and Sandra Phillips Gallery, Denver, CO.

Design: John Toren
ISBN: 978-1-947237-23-0

9 8 7 6 5 4 3 2

Library of Congress Control Number: 2019946598

AUTHOR'S NOTE
Most of the poems in this book were written between 2005 and 2019 with a few revised older strays thrown in. They are in no particular arrangement except some imagined order I saw at the time of publication.

Special thanks to Norton Stillman for agreeing to undertake this chaos and to John Toren for all his work.

Nodin Press
5114 Cedar Lake Road
Minneapolis, MN 55416
www.nodinpress.com

Printed in USA

for Ann

Contents

One

Two

Three

One

BIG BROWN PILLS

I believe in the big brown pills: they lower cholesterol and improve digestion. They help prevent cancer and build brain cells. Plus, they just make you feel better overall. I believe in coffee and beet greens and fish oil, of course, and red wine, in moderation, and cinnamon. Green tea is good and black tea and ginseng. I eat my broccoli. Nuts are very good, and dark chocolate—has to be dark, not milk chocolate. Tomatoes. But I think the big brown pills really help. I used to believe in the little yellow pills, but now I believe in the big brown pills. I believe that they are much more effective. I still take the little yellow ones, but I really believe in the big brown ones.

EARL

In Sitka, because they are fond of them, people have named the seal lions. Every sea lion is named Earl because they are killed one after another by the orca, the killer whale; sea lion bodies tossed left and right into the air. "At least he didn't get Earl," someone says. And sure enough, after a time, that same friendly, bewhiskered face bobs to the surface. It's Earl again. Well, how else are you to live except by denial, by some palatable fiction, some little song to sing while the inevitable, the black and white blindsiding fact, comes hurtling toward you out of the deep?

DEEP BLUE SEA

Every day I write in my notebook, at work on my book of poems that I will dedicate to you, even though you have gone away. I write, "Today the sea is as blue as your eyes." Or "The sea is not as blue as your eyes." Or "The sea is more blue than your eyes." Or "I am more blue than the sea, or than you, who are not blue at all except for your eyes"… The writing does not go well.

A DISAPPOINTMENT

The best anyone can say about you is that you are a disappointment. We had higher expectations for you. We had hoped that you would finish your schooling. We had hoped that you would have kept your job at the plant. We had hoped that you would have been a better son and a better father. We hoped, and fully expected, that you would finish reading *Moby Dick*. I wish that, when I am talking to you, you would at least raise your head off your desk and look at me. There are people who, without your gifts, have accomplished so much in this life. I am truly disappointed. Your parents, your wife and children, your entire family, in fact, everyone you know is disappointed, deeply disappointed.

BALONEY

There's a young couple in the parking lot, kissing. Not just kissing, they look as though they might eat each other up, kissing, nibbling, biting, mouths wide open, play fighting like young dogs, wrapped around each other like snakes. I remember that, sort of, that hunger, that passionate intensity. And I get a kind of nostalgic craving for it, in the way that I get a craving, occasionally, for the food of my childhood. Baloney on white bread, for instance: one slice of white bread with mustard or Miracle Whip or ketchup—not ketchup, one has to draw the line somewhere—and one slice of baloney. It had a nice symmetry to it, the circle of baloney on the rectangle of bread. Then you folded the bread and baloney in the middle and took a bite out of the very center of the folded side. When you unfolded the sandwich you had a hole, a circle in the center of the bread and baloney frame, a window, a porthole from which you could get a new view of the world.

LAW OF THE JUNGLE

We die of silliness, finally. Remember all those nights of wine, the heated discussion, the smoky room, the music? Those questions you pondered then have no relevance. "Why do we live?" you asked. More to the point now is, "Where do I live?" First you forget to zip; then, as time goes by, you forget to unzip. There is a banana peel around every corner. Remember all those powerful, intense things you said back then, how the girls found you powerful and intense? You couldn't say those things with a straight face now, and anyway, those girls weren't really listening. The old lion, with patchy mane and sagging belly, stands up to guard his territory. He gives a pathetic roar and the hyenas die laughing.

DON'T GET AROUND MUCH ANYMORE

"Barbara, it is so good to see you! How are you getting along since your divorce?"

"Why, Ellen, my divorce was twenty years ago! I'm fine."

"No! Twenty years, it can't have been that long?"

"Yes."

"How are your children?"

"They're both doing well, Jeff lives in Seattle and works for Microsoft. He and his wife have two boys, Evan and Lyle. Lyle is still in high school and Evan is in his second year at MIT studying engineering. Mara lives in Chicago and works for an ad agency. She's doing well, she and her partner are remodeling an old farmhouse near Oshkosh, so she's very busy, all that driving back and forth."

"And how about yourself, Barbara?"

"Oh, I'm very busy as well, work at the church, I work with the AAUW and I still play golf when I can."

"That's so good Barb! I think it's important to stay involved after a divorce. It's been so good to see you and remember, Barb, these things just take time."

ELDERLY MAN SHOT AND KILLED BY POLICE

"What shall we do with all these leftover Easter eggs? Make egg salad?" He says.

"I'm tired of egg salad," she says, "besides these are all cracked and dirty from the grandkids playing with them."

"We could throw them at cars," he says.

"That is a great idea!"

"I was kidding," he says.

"No seriously, It will be fun. I bet I can hit more than you."

"We have to try and hit the back of the car so the driver won't be too distracted."

According to a police statement, when the old man raised his hands he appeared to be holding what police thought to be a grenade. The object was later found to be an Easter egg.

The old man's last words to his wife were, "Did you hit any?"

"No," she said.

"Neither did I."

I SAW MAMA KISSING SANTA CLAUS

What neither junior nor his father knows is that she sees him every time he phones. The off-season, mostly. So it isn't true that Santa only comes once a year. She does her hair, her makeup, and puts on the little black dress he likes so much, and her heels. She goes to meet him in some little out-of-the-way joint downtown. It's difficult for a high-profile guy like Santa to be discreet. What does she see in him anyway? Overweight and god knows how old, red-faced, slack-jawed and snoring now in room 308 of the Seafarer's Hotel? Well, it's true, he can be fun, his humor and generosity are legendary. But she sees this can't last. Perhaps though, despite her slight feeling of disappointment and the obvious impossibility of the whole affair, she still holds out some faint hope. A belief in something wondrous about to happen, that somehow this year will be better than last.

COLORS

She said, "I see people as colors. My friend Jenny is yellow or gold." "Because she is blond?" "No it's not that. I think of James, for instance, as black, like a pirate flag, but his hair is quite blond." James was my rival, two years older and in college. "What color are you?" "Oh, I'm spring colors; maybe that bright green that you see when the leaves are still small. Kind of young and dumb." She laughed. She was so beautiful, her hair a wonderful red-gold and her eyes, I thought, green as the spring leaves. I knew I was getting nowhere. "What about me?" I asked. "What color am I?" "Oh, I see you as gray," she said, "shades of gray."

THE BIG BANG

When the morning comes that you don't wake up, what remains of your life goes on as some kind of electromagnetic energy. There's a slight chance you might appear on someone's screen as a dot. Face it. You are a blip or a ping, part of the background noise, the residue of the Big Bang. You remember the Big Bang, don't you? You were about 26 years old, driving a brand new red and white Chevy convertible, with that beautiful blond girl at your side, Charlene, was her name. You had a case of beer on ice in the back, cruising down Highway number 7 on a summer afternoon, and then you parked near Loon Lake just as the moon began to rise. Way back then you said to yourself, "Boy, it doesn't get any better than this," and you were right.

GRAVITY

It turns out that the drain pipe from the sink is attached to nothing and water just runs right onto the ground in the crawl space underneath the house and then trickles out into the stream that passes through the back yard. It turns out that the house is not really attached to the ground but sits atop a few loose concrete blocks all held in place by gravity, which, as I understand it, means "seriousness." Well, this is serious enough. If you look into it further you will discover that the water is not attached to anything either and that perhaps the rocks and the trees are not all that firmly in place. The world is a stage. But don't try to move anything. You might hurt yourself, besides that's a job for the stagehands and union rules are strict. You are merely a player about to deliver a soliloquy on the septic system to a couple dozen popple trees and a patch of pale blue sky.

CHAMELEON

I used to have a girlfriend named Jane Kieffer, from San Diego. She was beautiful and she was a chameleon. She could appear to be a small and waif-like blond or a tall redhead, to suit her whim, or mine. She would change her style, her look, her demeanor, almost instantly it seemed. She could be sophisticated or earthy, depending on my momentary needs, and the surroundings. She was fantastic, great at parties and when we were alone. She always knew just the right moves. The trouble was I didn't know what I wanted. It seemed, as a couple, we lacked any focus, any stability. She began to anticipate my moods and change in advance. It drove me crazy. "Who are you, why are you like this?" I asked. She said she was born in the sea and that she had no soul. "What about me?" "You have none either," she said. I was often angry and she would cry, or worse, sit impassively and say nothing, blending into the background. One day I pulled on my pants and said, "That's it. I'm leaving." I never saw her again—or else we got married and raised a family. I'm not sure.

INHERITANCE

My father came from nowhere in particular, and he was only distantly related to anyone, second cousin once removed. He came wearing a white suit, slammed into the hog pen when the brakes failed. The only things he owned were a few tools. He rose early. He went up and down the ladder, painting maroon or chartreuse, round and round the room in a sort of dance. He painted his face in a random pattern. Round and round till he fell down flat. I don't own the tools but I know some of the steps, some of the words to the song.

UNCLE AXEL

In the box of old photos there's one of a young man with a moustache wearing a long coat, circa 1890. The photo is labeled "Uncle Karl" on the back. That would be your mother's granduncle, who came from Sweden, a missionary, and was killed by Indians in North Dakota, your great-granduncle. The young man in the photo is looking away from the camera, slightly to the left. He has a look of determination, a man of destiny, preparing to bring the faith to the heathen Sioux. But it isn't Karl. The photo was mislabeled, fifty years ago. It's actually a photo of Uncle Axel, from Norway, your father's uncle, who was a farmer. No one knows that now. No one remembers Axel, or Karl. If you look closely at the photo it almost appears that the young man is speaking, perhaps muttering, "I'm Axel damn it. Quit calling me Karl!"

EXERCISE

Here is a Zen-inspired exercise for all you older guys. Dress comfortably in your shorts and a tee-shirt, hold your trousers in front of you with both hands, you will need to bend forward somewhat in order to hold your pants at knee level or below. Then while balancing on your right leg, lift your left leg and insert it into the left pant leg, repeat this process lifting your right and balancing on your left leg. See if you can do this without tipping over. Practice without using a chair or other support. This exercise is best done quickly and without thought. But, of course, now you have thought about it.

PARSIMONIOUS

What a luxury, what a gift to have had a life, more or less, my own, to wander, la-de-da, beneath the quaking aspen with leaves like $100 gold pieces and the blue, blue sky. And what shall I do with such riches? Give them away. Give them parsimoniously to family and friends, to those I love and those who love me, and give them in great abundance to strangers: thieves, con artists, drunks, politicians; wastrels like myself.

UNFORTUNATE LOCATION

In the front yard there are three big white pines, older than anything in the neighborhood except the stones. Magnificent trees that toss their heads in the wind like the spirited black horses of a troika. It's hard to know what to do, tall dark trees on the south side of the house, an unfortunate location, blocking the winter sun. Dark and damp. Moss grows on the roof, the porch timbers rot and surely the roots have reached the old bluestone foundation. At night, in the wind, a tree could stumble and fall, killing us in our beds. The needles fall year after year making an acid soil where no grass grows. We rake the fallen debris, nothing to be done. We stand around with sticks in our hands. Wonderful trees.

WHEN IT GETS COLD

When it gets cold around here we like to throw hot water into the air and watch it become instant ice mist that drifts away, never hitting the ground. Sometimes we drive nails with a frozen banana. Sometimes we just watch the numbers on the gas and the electric meters go spinning by. There's just no end to the fun.

But things get weird when it gets very cold. Things you never imagined come to life. There's an insect that appears, some kind of fly. Trees and houses make strange noises, and there are spooky, misty shapes moving around in the woods. Once when it was twenty-five below I found bare human footprints in snow that had fallen just a few hours before.

Everyone gets a little crazy when it's very cold for several weeks. Some people go in for compulsive house cleaning, others read, read everything: milk cartons, shipping labels ... We eat too much. We sleep a lot too. Once, during a cold spell, I slept for three days and when I woke I drank a gallon and a half of coffee.

PLANTING

I am not planting an acorn from which a mighty and symbolic oak will grow. There is no time for that now. I'll just plant a few seeds, a row of nasturtiums perhaps. I'm not looking for a career. I missed that. I just want a part-time job, nothing too strenuous. Because this isn't about growth or beauty or meaning, it's about the question of whether, at my age, having gotten down in the literal and metaphorical dirt, I can get up again.

BASEMENT

There's something about our basement that causes forgetting. I go down for something, say a roll of paper towels, which we keep in a big box down there, and as soon as I get to the bottom of the stairs I have forgotten what I came down there for. It happens to my wife as well. So recently we have taken to working in tandem like spelunkers. One of us stands at the top of the stairs while the other descends. When the descendant has reached the bottom stair, the person at the top calls out, "Light bulbs, 60 watt." This usually works unless the one in the basement lingers too long. I blame this memory loss on all the stuff in the basement. Too much baggage; 10 shades of blue paint, because we could not get the right color, extra dishes, bicycles, the washer and dryer, a cider press, a piano, jars of screws, nails and bolts … It boggles the mind. My wife blames it on radon.

BLACK BEARS

I like black bears. They are relatively common around here, and they are usually not aggressive. Actually, they are generally affable, loners mostly, but not opposed to hanging out with humans now and then. In fact, I've found that in many ways they are a lot like us.

My friend, Richard, an older male, drops by now and then and we hang out down on the shore, have a couple of beers, but mostly we just sit and look out at the water. We don't have a lot to say. We aren't friends exactly, but we enjoy the company. Richard says, at our age we don't have friends. We have associates.

LEGEND

As you grow older you begin to enter the world of myth, you become less a fact and more a legend. The word becomes flesh and then gradually becomes word once more. You exist mainly as the stories people tell about you, full of inconsistencies, inaccuracies, and downright lies. Anything else, what's really happening, isn't very interesting. But then, the stories most people tell aren't that good either. You can see this. The lives of the people you know become harder and harder to believe.

CLEAN UP

We invited some people over for drinks because they seemed nice and we thought it would be fun. They're about our age, a little younger maybe, and we have some things in common. They are coming this evening so now we have to clean the place up. What a drag. But we can't let them think that we are slobs, that we leave the morning oatmeal to dry hard in the pot, that the sink is full of yesterday's dirty dishes, that the kitchen table is piled high with books and magazines and coffee-stained papers, that the bed is unmade and the floor needs vacuuming. We can't let it appear that we are the kind of people who forget to change the car oil or mow the goddamn lawn; that we have completely lost our grip. We want them to know that we have not succumbed, that we can maintain order in the midst of all this chaos.

WHERE WE LIVE

It's easy to get lost in the woods around here, to wander around in circles, not 50 feet away from the path, and never see it. Beneath the canopy of trees not even your GPS will work. It leads to a lot of uncertainty. So if you come to visit I can't be very specific with my directions. I can only give you probabilities. We leave a lot of notes around as indicators: "Dentist Thur. 9:30," "Eggs," "Pick up Mom." It doesn't always work. "Honey, what's this blank Post-It note stuck to the bathroom mirror all about?" "Oh, nothing," she says.

THE PERSONAL HISTORY CHANNEL

For a few dollars more a month you can add the Personal History Channel to your cable package. You can then while away the hours, reviewing the stupid and embarrassing things you did in years gone by. It can be fascinating watching yourself learning to ride a bicycle or going on your first date. When you come to more recent times, however, there are more and more shows that feature you sitting on the couch, eating chips and watching the Personal History Channel.

A PLACE OF YOUR OWN

It is so good to have a place of your own, a comfortable bed, a place where in the evening you can hide away from all the defeat of the day, a place where you know where things are, or at least you know in which pile a particular item might be found. But suppose one day the place gets ransacked while you are away. Maybe you're lucky, maybe it was only the three bears, but the place is a mess, your neat stack of L.L. Bean catalogs strewn all over. They've eaten everything; even that jar of pickled Brussels spouts way at the back of the fridge. Even after you get it all cleaned up it's not the same as it was. "You have to move on," a friend of mine says, "at our age we can just close the door and go away, take a trip to China or Hot Springs. Just think of it as practice for not being here at all."

THE PAINTER

After he has covered the earth the painter is ready to start on the sky. Beauty requires constant attention and, anyway, it's a living. What color is the sky today? Blue. He stirs the paint, pours half into his bucket and starts up the ladder one step at a time, slowly. He climbs above the trees, above the cows grazing in the field, above the rivers and mountains. He leans to one side and spits—a long way down. He doesn't like it much. He hooks his bucket to the ladder and dips his brush. He makes the first even stroke.

HERITAGE

Great-grandmother Murphy was a proud woman. She came from a well-to-do family that had connections back east. She had presence and bearing. Great-Grandpa Murphy was an Irishman of dubious ancestry and background. Nevertheless they got married, as people do. Grandpa Murphy shuffled along as they walked downtown, looking at the ground or his feet. He found things that way: an Indian arrowhead, sometimes a nickel or a dime. A dime was worth something in those days. And here is a perfectly good comb, just needs to be boiled a bit to kill the bugs. Grandmother kept her head high as she walked along; she was a Smith, after all, one of *the* Smiths. But she never found anything.

THE LEARNING CURVE

There are certain concepts that I only vaguely understand but that people talk about all the time. You frequently hear the term "learning curve," for instance. I suppose that refers to how one learns a new skill or gains knowledge over a period of time, described as an ascending arc from zero (knowing nothing) to ten, the zenith (knowing all there is to know about a thing). Then comes the gradual descent, the arc of forgetting, back to zero. Then, feet firmly planted on the ground in the batting box of ignorance, the learning curve ball comes whistling past and slowly you come to understand that once again you are out.

Two

MY ANCESTRAL HOME

We came to a beautiful little farm. From photos I'd seen I knew this was the place. The house and barn were painted in the traditional Falu red, trimmed with white. It was nearly midsummer, the trees and grass, lush green. When we arrived the family was gathered at a table on the lawn for coffee and fresh strawberries. Introductions were made all around, Grandpa Sven, Lars-Olaf and Marie, Eric and Gudren, Cousin Inge and her two children ... It made me think of a Carl Larsen painting. But, of course, it was all modern, the Swedes are very up-to-date, Lars-Olaf was an engineer for Volvo, and they all spoke perfect English, except for Grandpa, and there was a great deal of laughter over my attempts at Swedish. We stayed for a long time laughing and talking, it was late in the day but the sun was still high. I felt a wonderful kinship. It seemed to me that I had known these people all my life, they even looked like family back in the States. But as it turned out we had come to the wrong farm. Lars-Olaf said, "I think I know your people, they live about three miles from here. If you like I could give them a call." I said that no, that it wasn't necessary, this was close enough.

HITCHHIKERS

I pick up bull thistles and burdock, beggar ticks, cockle-burs, sandburs, seeds of all sorts, on my pants legs as I walk the fields and ditches. Somewhere, way down the road, some will fall on fertile ground and begin the haphazard garden all over again. I pick up pebbles in my shoe treads and when they fall out they spawn streambeds, glacial eskers, mountain ranges. One day there will be a huge boulder right where your house is now, but it will take awhile.

FREEZE

Everything in the garden is dead, killed by a sudden hard freeze, the beans, the tomatoes, fruit still clinging to the branches. It's all heaped up ready to go to the compost pile: rhubarb leaves, nasturtiums, pea vines, even the geraniums. It's too bad. The garden was so beautiful, green and fresh, but then we were all beautiful once. Everything dies, we understand. But the mind of the observer, which cannot imagine not imagining, goes on. The dynasties are cut down like the generations of grass, the bodies blacken and turn into coal. The waters rise and cover the earth and the mind broods on the face of the deep, and learns nothing.

AS IS

We've sold the house so we have to move. Now I don't have to think about cutting down that old ugly silver maple tree. I don't have to worry about the squirrels in the attic or mowing the lawn. Not my problem. I intend to blow away like the fluff from a dandelion. One of the last things I'll do before we leave is to drag the old Adirondack chair out to the street corner to be hauled away by anyone who wants it. Sinister device! Sit down there and you may never be able to get up again.

SUPERVISOR

They have knocked down the old school, across the street, bulldozed the little woods nearly out of existence. They are putting up new shops and building affordable housing for students and seniors. All day the trucks and front-end loaders are at work filling the air with dust and noise. I sit and watch as if I were some kind of supervisor. People walk by and say, "How's it going?" "Great," I say. "Right on schedule."

WORLDLY GOODS

I've sold or given away most of my books and my tools, and most of my fishing gear and my canoe. I have only one rod and reel left, so some days I sit and fish and some days I just sit. There is a certain satisfaction in the divesting of worldly goods, as there is in quitting a job, a kind of spiritual release, a sanctimony. And every day I feel that I become more Godlike, in that soon, like God, I won't do anything at all.

EVOLUTION

I think it's okay not to like the idea of evolution. I can understand how one would not like to think of oneself as distantly related to a lemur, since most of us are none too fond of some of our more immediate relatives. But it seems to me that evolution is the least of our worries. For years I have accepted things as they are, or seem to be, without thinking much about them. Not now. Now, I have come to realize that I don't approve of gale-force winds or high water, or volcanoes or earthquakes. The idea of tectonic plates doesn't appeal to me. The idea that we are dependent on gravity to keep us on the ground makes me queasy—the idea that there is no up or down and we are merely sticking out from the planet. I don't at all like the idea of flight, except for birds. I don't even enjoy riding in automobiles. I believe, even though I do not practice it, that we should walk everywhere we go. But then there's the problem of standing, balance and all that. I'm not so sure that just two legs is a good idea.

AFTERNOON IN NICE

for Walt Cannon

It must have been France, or Belgium. No it had to be
France ... Nice, at a sidewalk café, pigeons walking about
under the tables. It was a warm day. Sun. The girls in
their summer dresses. I was speaking fluent French and
joked with the waiters who responded in French. The
problem was that I had no understanding of what they
were saying or for that matter, what I was saying, but that
has been a problem all along. It all worked out, I guess,
because in the end I was served a large bowl of moules et
frites and a glass of wine.

CLOUD ATLAS

– Eh! qu'aimes-tu donc, extraordinaire etranger?
– J'aime les nuages... les nuages qui passent...
la-bas... la-bas... les merveilleux nuages!

– Baudelaire

I. Cumulus

One lives in the world more quietly, sometimes, than one would like. And yes, beyond this world is another. One lives with that world too, as with a crazy uncle who comes downstairs occasionally for whiskey and cigarettes, then it's back up to his room where he's working on a plan of significance to the world at large. Thinking ... It's quiet. He's right though, beyond this second world is yet another. World piles on world in a compact and towering mass that, with its domes and canyons, resembles a cauliflower or the human brain.

Each moment, though it passes silently, is a turmoil of emotions, our smallest actions driven by workings more complex than those of a watch but less precise.

(I lean toward you over the piña coladas as our conversation drifts from the international monetary crisis to your favorite music.)

We expect certain grace with all this energy the way the *Arethusa*, under Liberian registry, slides across the oily water to her berth easily, swiftly ... a little too swiftly perhaps ... Full Astern! White water boils up behind, seagulls fly away ... Too late. There will be an investigation, the captain relieved of his command. We give names to the winds aloft and expect them to arrange everything. Because of Love a man will leave his home and spend the rest of his life in Pittsburgh. It's frightening.

One thing leads to another. Pomp and Circumstance. Great cumulus clouds pass slowly through the summer sky like parade floats. And the slender grasses gather round you, pressing forward, with exaggerated deference, whispering, eager to catch a glimpse. It's your party after all. And it couldn't be more perfect. Yet there's a nagging thought: you don't really deserve all this attention, and that, come October, there will be a price to pay.

II. Stratus

Everywhere you look are the poor, the old and sick, those who must count the cost of everything, each tooth, each hair numbered, each icy step a risk, those for whom one and one and one add up to nothing, no horizon, a shuffling walk from bed to window where the muted light plays on the building next door.

Today air and water have fused, no lake, no sky, no horizon … an apartment wall. A Kline poster, books, cinder blocks and boards, teapot, frying pan, coffee cups … the dishes pile up in the sink. The faucet drips, drips as grey afternoon ticks into evening.

A woman moves in perhaps, bringing curtains, a rug, a couple of geckos. But you, preoccupied, listen to the careful tick, tick considering the possible combinations waiting for the tumblers to fall.

The colors are black and white or combinations thereof. The answers are yes and no, yes no yes, no no no and yes or maybe when seen from a distance. From here it is possible to think in the grandest terms yet someone walking just behind you has disappeared between one and zero.

III. Cirrus

It seems to me you enjoyed shattering the fine bone china though the focus of our discussion escapes me. Perhaps there was a wisp of hair that curled in front of your left eye that you brushed back as you spoke. I've forgotten because I kissed you, probably, and took your hand awhile. Beneath that translucent skin the tiny veins branch to invisible capillaries: the ancient delta culture bred to a fine nervous instability. Perhaps so much detail left us confused, confounded by a superfluity of information: shoe sizes, opinions about Nietzsche ...

One wearies of matters of substance, I recommend those moments that, without reason, last a lifetime: that beautiful red-haired girl on the shore brushing her teeth as we sailed away, a glimpse of a face, a shoulder in a doorway; moments like music, truth untroubled by meaning. Of course, there's not, at this altitude, enough oxygen for a swallow, let alone a family of four.

That first glimpse, as the plane turned, of the Sangre de Cristos with their lacework of snow set against the western sky, patterns repeated in cloud, in sand, in sun on water all seemed, somehow, like mileposts on the true way, indicators of something that would finally reveal itself. Yet, at any moment the wind could peel back the pie-crust aluminum exposing the sham, the skein of wire, the ridiculous construct of kitchenware and string that could not, under any circumstance, allow for flight. And yet we seem to be moving right along.

LIFE IN THE WOODS

The woods around you have grown up sheerly to depress you with their dampness and dark. The small birds have all flown away, leaving you alone in the gloom. For a point of reference there's a pile of rusted cans and broken bottles. For company there are mosquitoes. If you call out for help you are put on hold.

If you live long enough in the forest, the forest people, some so old and bent over that their long noses touch the ground, the hidden ones, those conversant with the moon and the devil and the west wind, may come in the night once or twice a month and clean your bathroom. Or not. Which means they don't like you.

SIT DOWN

I often spend a good portion of each day wandering all about trying to find the right place to sit down. The place you choose to sit must be the right height, not too low because of the difficulty of rising again. An Adirondack chair is a bad choice, as is a canoe. I know of two or three rocks along the shore of Lake Superior that I find to be of a comfortable height and good for a short stay. Hardness is another factor. Sofas are usually a bad choice, especially if it's your girlfriend's parent's sofa. Don't sit on the edge of a bed. Chairs in the dentist's office waiting room are always uncomfortable. Actually, an overturned bucket overlooking a hole in the ice is probably better, but not by much.

On a sunny day in late March or early April you can get yourself a good sturdy straight-backed chair and go to the south side of the shack, sit down and lean back, chair and all, against the sun-warmed tarpaper wall. You've got the back legs of the chair planted in the snow for extra support. You can just doze there, while the sunlight soaks into the black paper-covered wall, and into you, and you soak into the black background, deeper and deeper until you disappear.

DRINKING ALONE

Because I have no one else to drink with tonight I go down to the lakeshore and take the water and the moon for my companions. Already the moon is high and the water, stirred by the wind, becomes loquacious. It's the same old story. The water sculpts these rocks. It takes a thousand years, smoothing and polishing. There's no money in it, so far from the major markets. As I listen I grow drowsy. Water on the rocks ... What's to be done ... What's to be done?

OCTOBER (ABOVE LAKE SUPERIOR)

A north wind shakes the last few yellow leaves clinging to a thin popple tree. It's easy to tell what's coming. Old leaves must fall to make way for the new. That's all well and good as long as it's not your turn to go. Keep the dead waiting! Keep the unborn waiting! There's not much to this life anyway, some notions, some longings that come and go like the sea, like sun and shadow played across the stone. This weather is not so bad if you can find a place among the rocks in the sun and out of the wind.

TRAVELS

Almost every day I go down to the lakeshore to sit and watch the waves roll in and I am filled with the same old restlessness, the urge to move on ... but where? There is nothing between here and Texas but prairie towns, ethanol plants, and bad Mexican restaurants ... the vagrant dust.

Still, there are places I could go, but where? The Middle East? Definitely not. Not India, China, Russia or Paraguay. Not Antarctica. I once heard of a poet who was awarded a prize, a two-week stay in Antarctica. I think second prize must have been three weeks in Antarctica. I don't want to go to the Amazon, the Congo or any tropical rain forest. In fact in most places there are too many people, and/or other nasty species. I have no desire to see a Komodo dragon or the deadly Irukandji jellyfish. But there was someplace I wanted to go, someplace ... I just can't think where right now.

SEAGULLS

There were no seagulls in the harbor, none at the marina. I saw none in the air. There were no seagulls at Canal Park, or McDonald's, or at Russ Kendall's smokehouse, or at the Kmart parking lot, or any of their favorite hangouts. It's winter and snow is falling, but I don't believe seagulls fly south. I've often seen them standing around on the ice all day, as if they were waiting for a big bus to come and take them to a casino. Where are all the seagulls? This is not a question I ever thought I'd ask myself. You get used to someone being around and if they go away you miss them. That's how life is. But seagulls are primarily a nuisance, and if you can't count on that, what can you count on?

LARGE DOG

A dog would be the thing, she thought, now that she lived alone, a big dog that looked rather scary and barked, a watchdog, but one that was actually gentle, a companion, a big, lovable fur ball. She adopted a dog from the pound, Cosmo, who was part German shepherd and part golden retriever. She got all his shots and had him neutered. She got a retractable leash for walks, morning and evening, after work. Walk time. Cosmo is happy, sniffing and pulling this way and that. She calls and pulls back. She has a big dog on a leash but she is going where he wants to go.

STARFISH

It seems like starfish don't do anything, but actually they move along at a rate of about 60 feet per hour. A starfish will eat anything that moves slower than it does, which excludes a great number of dishes from its diet. A starfish is all arms and appetite; it has no brain, yet in spite of this, time-lapse photography has shown that the starfish maintains an active social life. So in these regards the starfish is like many of the people you know.

NEW SHOES

Because I'm in Europe, I've been thinking of buying some European shoes. European shoes do not look quite like American shoes. You look at someone's shoes and say to yourself, "those are European shoes. They are made of leather, the toes are more pointy, or more square, or … something … they are just different." In America we mostly wear tennis shoes. We have casual tennis shoes, formal tennis shoes, even tennis shoes for tennis. Over here it is different, but my eye is not practiced enough to determine if the shoes vary from country to country. If that is the case, and since all shoes are made in China, think how confusing it must be for the Chinese worker packaging up the shoes for shipment, looking at a pair of loafers, scratching his or her head and wondering, "Do these shoes go to Luxembourg or Hungary?" In China, as we all know, everyone wears silk bedroom slippers.

SANDALS

I never really feel comfortable wearing sandals. They don't seem right for this northern climate. Up here we are always expecting it to turn cold. We never go anywhere without a jacket. So when it gets warm enough to wear sandals, usually four or five days in early August, it feels as though I'm taking a big risk to do so. Sandals make me realize how vulnerable I am, nothing at all to protect my toes from falling rocks or scalding hot water. If you wear sandals your feet are available to mosquitoes and wood ticks and other vermin. You don't want to walk into the woods wearing sandals; you don't want to play soccer or rugby. I feel more at ease in boots and wool socks, but every summer I wear my sandals once or twice as an indicator that I'm not planning to do anything at all.

ON KARL JOHAN'S GATE

On Karl Johan's Gate, at a street corner, there is a man and a woman arguing in a language I have never heard before. It is a bitter argument. It is possible that they are the only two people in all of Norway who speak this language, they have come a long way, it has been difficult, but they have arrived, at last, on a street corner in Oslo, and now they are lost.

WORRY BEADS

for Dennis Matson

The hand is held outward, away from the body in the gesture of one about to shake the hand of another. The string of worry beads is held between the first and second fingers, at approximately the middle joint of the fingers. The string is attached to a loop of metal beads, which hangs down on the outside of the hand. The loop is flipped up and over the hand with a quick outward motion of the little finger and without turning the wrist. The beads now hang on the inside of the hand. They are now flipped back to their original position with the thumb. Thus to (theoretically) relieve tension and anxiety this action is repeated rapidly many times. After repeated attempts I find I am unable to do this and it worries me.

SAVE THE PLANET

It makes no difference to the earth, the earth is fine, carbon dioxide, carbon monoxide, kudzu or tumbleweeds, an abundance of life, or none, life goes on, or not, and it makes no difference to the planet. It's we who care ... or we don't. No more pork belly, no more catfish, no gin at the 18th hole, no more wallowing in the buffalo wallow, no more baby buffalos. No difference. Who cares if Jack manages to buy his chain of car washes? Not me.

SUITCASE

I keep my clothes in a suitcase at the foot of my bed. I haven't been anywhere and have no plans to go anywhere, but these days you never know, and besides it gives me a focus for my anxiety and for my occasional moments of unfounded excitement and anticipation. Every morning I take out clean socks and underwear, etc. and throw the dirty clothes back in the suitcase. Once a week or so I take the suitcase down to the washer and dryer in the basement and sit around naked waiting for my clean clothes. That's about it. The days pass quickly enough. Once in awhile I see old friends. "You look tired," they say or "Why the long face?" I reply, "Well, you know, it's stressful, living out of a suitcase."

COMPLETE STRANGERS

These days I find it hard to remember which of my contemporaries are dead and which are still alive. But to tell the truth when I meet them on the street or in the grocery store the dead ones don't look that much worse than the living, and none of them has much to say. Mostly, we have found it mutually advantageous to ignore one another, pretending not to see, or that we are complete strangers, and the years pass and eventually we forget entirely. But occasionally there may come one of those awkward moments, at a party or someplace, when our host says, "Art, have you met Elwin?" And there is one of my long dead acquaintances. "Oh, yes," I say, shaking Elwin's hand, "we're old friends, we go back a long way." Then, sometime later I wonder, "Now, what was that guy's name?"

BOWERBIRD

The satin bowerbird builds his bower carefully, a construction of twigs and grass, and carefully decorates it with display items, blue feathers, blue bottle caps, blue bits of paper and potsherds. His feathers are blue and he likes blue, and more to the point, the female bowerbird likes blue. During the mating season the bower is constantly rearranged and rebuilt. The bower isn't a nest, it's an elaborate construction designed to lure female bowerbirds. So it's like theoretical physics or poetry, hard work and essentially useless, except for the sex. And in most cases the female bowerbird doesn't even take a second look at what she considers to be a second-rate bower. She has an eye. She knows immediately a bower worthy of her close inspection. The bower builder is preening and doing his little song and dance. "You wouldn't believe how far I had to fly with that bottle cap in my beak." She likes the look of this bower, likes the way those twigs are arranged, just so. Likes the little touches of red plastic, here and there among the blue things. Yes, this is a bird that can build a better bower, should she ever need one. So perhaps she'll just step inside.

HAIRCUT

Shall I wait to get my haircut after my hair has gotten too long, have it cut too short and await the day, the hour, when my hair reaches its perfect length? Or should I have it cut often, keeping my coif constantly at its optimum length? That becomes expensive and besides I like to live in anticipation of the moment. But the moment passes so quickly. For instance, there must have been a period in my life when I was at my peak. Maybe it was only a year or so when, at last, I got my act together, maybe for only a few weeks, or days, when my mental and physical powers were at their fullest. Maybe it was only a couple of hours in the early morning of some forgotten day and I slept through the whole thing. And when I woke things had begun to deteriorate.

PINE SISKINS

All aggression and appetite, they fight for space at the feeder, ruffling and flapping. Such rudeness from so delicate a bird. The weight ratio of brain to body enhances their capacity for flight but limits their talent for reflection and conjecture. They live out their daily lives in instinctual confusion, dropping several seeds for every one they eat. It's a folly that serves a need, feeding a squirrel, rabbit or mouse. One male sidesteps toward a female and she sidesteps away but not very far. Some unseen signal, some slight movement or sound, sends the entire flock into the air; each bird held perfectly aloft, unencumbered by engines of faith.

DUCKS

There are two types of ducks, divers and dabblers. Divers feed on fish, plants and insects in deep water. They live on big lakes and rivers. Dabblers prefer shallow water, ponds and creeks where they feed on plants and insects. Dabblers are also known as puddle ducks. Once, on a very rainy day, I saw a mallard land on water that had accumulated in the street, not more than 6 or 7 inches deep. If I decided to be a duck I'd probably choose to be a dabbler, it's more my nature, dabbling here and there, farting around, not like a diver, some sharp-billed merganser intent on something lurking in the deep. And unlike the diving ducks who need a long runway to become airborne, running and flapping along the surface of the water, dabblers take off from the water with a sudden, upward leap into the air.

OUT OF IT

I'm out of it these days. I guess I have less interest in keeping up to date on what's happening. I don't know the names of most of the current movie stars and have not seen their movies. Same for the music scene. I have not read what everyone is reading. I don't know what's on TV. I'm out of it, but not too far out. I figure somewhere between 12 to 18 inches. I've noticed that when someone speaks to me he or she seems to be addressing a space just a little to my right or left. When it first happened I thought my acquaintance was speaking to someone else. I looked around but there was no one else there. I've tried moving to adjust the conversational direction but the speaker only readjusts. I realized that if I kept moving our conversation would be going in circles. So now I just stand still and let the talk continue at cross-purposes. It is getting worse. Sometimes I can't make any sense at all of what someone is saying, as if he were speaking Welsh. Then I remember that I am in Wales and he *is* speaking Welsh.

FEVER

I am being interviewed for the job of Area Representative. I am flying over the tundra at 250 mph., my nose and fingertips not more than three inches above the ice.

I wake to discover that the glasses and bottles on the table by the bed have crowded together, waiting to be taken across the river.

A pen with an extremely fine point is signing on a tiny scrap of paper my name over and over again. It is all perfectly clear.

I have never really noticed the things in this room. I have been unaware of their articulations: the longings of the chest, the desires of the bed, the faint groaning of the walls at night, those obscure concessions the house makes to the earth, settling.

The room is quiet now, everything falling at the same rate of speed.

GET IT DONE

A lot of heat is produced by the intensity of people trying to get things done. It leads to speeding, tailgating, uneven tire wear, cost overruns, ill considered attire ... The ground is littered with abandoned projects, the telegraph, the Erie Canal ... The wheels spin, the grease begins to smoke, the bearings burn up, the wheels fall off and the whole thing is on fire. All the heat produced by this fervor only leads to global warming. Suppose the economy doesn't recover? It's a minor inconvenience. Or a meteor hits the earth? That might cause a lot of initial problems, but in the long run it might do many trillion dollars worth of good.

THE WOODS IN FALL

In the city it seems no one treats you as a human being. The woods, on the other hand, are full of things that do, that run if you come too close. It's lonely. Who will I talk to? Who will I invite to my birthday party? Bears tend to overindulge and fall asleep. Alfred, the great gray owl, commonly known as Al Owl, can never remember anyone's name ... The days are bright and the nights clear and cold. Most all the leaves have fallen by now, the red and orange maple, the yellow birch and poplar. Only the somber evergreens are unmoved. If I clear a few of the dead leaves from this little pool there is the perfect sky again, on the other side, and a face, not quite mine, but that apes my every move and refuses to go away until I do.

THE TENT

Concave on the windward side, convex on the lee, it snaps and strains the ropes. Green nylon not quite the color of the forest, it is the flag of nothing in particular, a banner that proclaims we will not be here very long, a modest shelter shedding only the lightest rains. Like home anywhere, pitched on an unsheltered point, the tent wants to fly into the air, heave sideways into the lake.

SMALL FISH

He's too small to keep so I remove the hook and put him back in the water. He hesitates a moment near the surface, as if not quite realizing where he is, then with a swift movement of the tail he's gone. He's back in it now, his own deep blue-green, the daily hunger and panic. He has no way of thinking about this experience. He was, then he was not, and now he is again. A seizure. But then, moments later, he's back on the surface a few feet from the boat, lying on his side, the gills working, one in the water, one in the useless air. He'd hit the bait hard and the hook had gone in deep—youthful folly, you could say, or extreme hunger, or plain bad luck. I reach out and try to grab him, but he's still too quick even in this condition. He swims down again. He's determined but the water will not have him any more. In a few seconds he's back, farther from the boat, in the domain of sunlight and hungry seagulls.

THE SILK ROAD

We wouldn't have to go home. We could go on from here to Istanbul, then to Ankara and Tabriz, over the Silk Road. It will probably take months, years maybe, on foot or camelback to reach Xian. We'd go through Theran, Asgabat, Bukhara, Samarkand, Tashkent, Kashgar, Turphan, Hami, Anxi, Lanzhou. Across deserts, rivers and mountains. We'd see the Great Wall, Maiji Mountain, Jiayuguan Pass, Wuwei Confucius Temple. It worries me a bit that we have nothing to trade. The Chinese have silk, gunpowder ... They like horses I guess ... Maybe we could pick up some frankincense and myrrh along the way but I'm not exactly where you get that stuff or if I'd know it when I saw it. I don't see this as a big problem though, we'll just go along and things will occur as they occur. Tonight ... perhaps Venice or Trieste.

REGRET

There's no use in regret. You can't change anything. Your mother died unhappy with the way you turned out. You and your father were not on speaking terms when he died, and you left your wife for no good reason. Well, it's past. You may as well regret missing out on the conquest of Mexico. That would have been just your kind of thing back when you were eighteen: a bunch of murderous Spaniards, out to destroy a culture and get rich. On the other hand, the Aztecs were no great shakes either. It's hard to know whom to root for in this situation. The Aztecs thought they had to sacrifice lots of people to keep the sun coming up every day. And it worked. The sun rose every day. But it was backbreaking labor, all that sacrificing. The priests had to call in the royal family to help, and their neighbors, the gardener, the cooks ... You can see how this is going to end. You are going to have your bloody, beating heart ripped out, but you are going to have to stand in line, in the hot sun, for hours, waiting your turn.

NO MATTER HOW FAR YOU DRIVE

I sat between Mamma and Daddy.
My sister sat on Mamma's lap.
Daddy drove. Fields, telephone poles ...
I watched the sun go down.
"Never look straight at the sun,
it could ruin your eyes."
No matter how far you drive
you can't get to the sun.
I touched the pearly knob
of the gearshift lever
and felt the vibration in my fingers.
It made Daddy nervous.
"Never mess around with that.
You could ruin the car,
cause an accident."
It was dark, the sun gone to China.
Out there in the dark,
fourteen lights. I counted. Fourteen.
Rabbits ran in front of the car
from one black ditch to the other.
I didn't know where we were.
I could see the red light on the dashboard
and the light of Daddy's Lucky Strike
that broke into a million sparks behind us
when he threw it out the window.

Three

STARRY STARRY NIGHT

A bazillion stars overhead, and I look up as amazed and baffled as the first hominid who gazed upward must have been, stars passing overhead like a very slow-moving flock of birds, going somewhere, disappearing into the wee hours of the morning. I used to be able to recognize some of the constellations: the Pleiades, the Big Dipper ... but I have forgotten most. Still, mankind has learned a lot about the cosmos since Galileo's time. A friend of mine said, "My wife bought me a telescope for my birthday, a nice one, very powerful, I've got it set up on the deck. You know, when you look at a star with your naked eye all you see is a little white dot, but when you look at it through a telescope you see a bigger white dot."

ART

I decided that it would be nice to be someone else for a change. I call myself Art. Being someone else is kind of like having a guest, so my job is to make Art feel welcome and happy. What would Art like? Art would like coffee, I think, so off I go. When I meet someone I say "How do you do? Name's Art." If I meet someone I know already they say, "Your name is Lou, not Art, you have always been Lou." "Oh, all right then, call me Lou." (Art is a very easy-going guy.) I just don't see why people have to be so inflexible, so unequivocal, so... definite. Meanwhile, I have learned that Art likes baseball, so I've got a ticket to this afternoon's Twins game.

I MUST SAY

Now that we have come so far together, so much water gone under the bridge, and now that the shadows lengthen around us, I feel that I must say some things that are difficult for me to say … This is a world of plague-bearing prairie dogs and freshly fried flesh. Where is the fish sauce shop, and when did the Irish wristwatch shop shut? Are our oars oak? Are the sheep asleep in the shed? I cannot give you specific statistics but surely the sun will shine soon. Surely the sun will shine on the stop signs and on the twin-screw steel cruisers.

I have lain awake nights thinking of how to say this. I can only hope that what these words lack in meaning will be somehow compensated for by your understanding of my need to say them, and by your knowing that these words are meant for you. Though who you are in this context is never made clear, and it is quite possible that you, yourself, do not know.

CULT FOLLOWING

Like most poets my poems never got much attention. They were hardly ever reviewed in literary magazines (which nobody reads anyway) or anywhere, for that matter. But, I still have a few readers scattered here and there, across the country. I like to think of them as a cult following. Perhaps they have a way of recognizing each other, a secret handshake, a wink, a raised eyebrow, whatever ... a group of eccentrics and misfits. I like to imagine that they gather at a designated place deep in the oak forest, at this time of year when the leaves are all nearly down and the moon is full. They build a big bonfire, have a few drinks, read a poem or two of mine aloud, maybe they sing a song, and end by throwing copies of my books into the fire.

WISHES

Wishes, if they come true, always have a way of turning out badly. The fisherman's wife got wealth and power but wound up with nothing. Tithonus was given eternal life by Zeus but not eternal youth so the gift had unpleasant consequences. King Midas did not do well with his wish either. Solomon wished for wisdom, got wealth and power besides and still was not a happy man. Suppose you wished to be far away from the stupid, repressive town you grew up in and suddenly you were whirled away in a cloud of dust. Before long some well-intentioned fool would miss you and wish you home again. If you wished for a beautiful woman or rich and handsome husband you *know* what would happen. What *is* there to wish for finally? A blindfold and a last cigarette? No, we all know how bad smoking is for your health. When the genie comes out of the bottle or the man comes to your door with a check the size of a billboard you should say "No." "No thank you." Say, "I don't want any." Say, "I wish you would go away." But you aren't going to, are you?

AMULET

for Ann

My wife comes to my chair. She is in her nightgown. "Goodnight" she says and gives me a kiss. "Just in case," she adds. I think she means "in case I fall asleep before you come to bed." But the possibilities are endless. Just in case the roof falls in from the weight of the snow and we are killed in our beds, or Yellowstone explodes, or suppose America elects a psychopathic moron as president. It is a kind of amulet to protect against illness, pain and poverty; the gathering storm. It's worked (more or less) for us for more than forty years. Just in case, one kiss and goodnight.

MAGNUM OPUS

Back then, I wrote all the time, I wrote like a madman, and I was, of course, alone in my dingy little apartment with the nearby freight trains rattling the windows all night long, accentuating my loneliness. It was love, unrequited passion. Nowadays, my ardor cooled somewhat by the years, I write down lines on little scraps of paper and if I come across them, weeks or months, maybe even years later, (the way time goes) they may become part of the magnum opus, or maybe not. I can foresee the time when I will cease to bother with paper and pencils, a more eco-friendly method, and just formulate and arrange the words in my head, and then, later maybe, not even that. Perhaps then the thoughts, the unformed notions will arrive and pass by like birds or wisps of clouds, leaving the sky clear and blue.

AWAKE AT NIGHT

They lie awake for an hour or more, motionless, neither speaking, under their covers making a shape like two low hills or like two long gray clouds that roll in on an afternoon in late fall. Perhaps they will lie like this, side by side, after death, silent until she says, "What time is it?" And he says, "2093."

Maybe she wants to talk. She says, "I'm having a lot of trouble with Photoshop CS3." And he says, "I don't want to talk about software right now." She snuggles close and says, "Do you want to talk about hardware then?"

THE LONG WINTER

The winter here is so long that one needs to find an outdoor activity to pass the time. Some people ski or snowboard. There's snowmobiling, ice skating, hockey ... I prefer ice fishing. Standing around in the cold wind all day, pulling ice fish from a hole in the ice. Ice fish have to be eaten raw, like sushi. If you cook an ice fish you wind up with nothing but a skillet full of water. Gnash one down or swallow it whole, there is nothing like the flavor, full of the glittering, bitter cold of a January day. Your teeth crack, your tongue goes numb, your lips turn blue and your eyes roll back in your head. "God!" you say, "God that was good! Let me have just one more."

DARK MATTER

I just hope that when I die I am really dead. I don't want to be someplace, to be me waiting for something, waiting, sitting in an uncomfortable chair filling out papers. I don't want to meet with a supreme being or this being's amanuensis. I don't want to look from beyond at the ten thousand things, to see things I hate, war, poverty, politicians ... Or the things I like but can no longer have: barbeque ribs, whisky, wind in the trees, birds flying, sunsets across the water, brown paper packages tied up with string, toast and butter ... and of course you, my honey. At most I hope to be a particle, or a part of a particle. Something with no memory, no agenda ... a minor probability.

LIGHTNING

I'm too old and too stupid to write poems anymore. Not that you need to be especially smart to write a poem. You just have to have the knack, to be able to recognize that moment when your hair stands on end, that moment when you are in proximity of lightning. That doesn't occur very often, the time when you get that flash and boom. It hardly ever happens to me anymore. That's for younger people ... Still, I know of several people, around my age, whom I wish would be struck by lightning. Real lightning.

WINTER DAY

It is one of those dark winter days with a heavy snow falling. I start to move a chair from its place in the corner and suddenly realize someone had been sitting there in the shadows all along. "Oh! I'm sorry!" "Oh, no problem," he says, as he jumps up. I try replacing the chair, but it's no use. He stands at the window, hands folded behind his back, watching the snow fall in the yard. "Would you like some tea?" "No, no, I'm fine." I feel as though I should know this person; that he is here out of some courtesy to me. "This snow is really coming down," he says. "Yes," I say. "I should be going before the roads get too bad." He stands at the window and does not move. "Yes," I say.

ILLUSION

Is it true that this world, this life, is an illusion, all smoke and mirrors? It must be, because according to a recent poll, seventy percent of the American public believes that Ronald Reagan did a good job as president. And yet if life is only a figment, a feint, a construction of breath and vapor, then why is it a rock falls and smashes your toe and you go hopping around on one foot, mad with pain? Why, if you happen to look at a woman on the sidewalk and your car plows into the truck in front of you, are you dead and no longer allowed to play the game? It's an illusion, but it's a damn good one.

TANGO

In a relationship like this there is one who does not really care, and that forces the other into the position of the one who does: positive and negative forces, so that things will go around. A Tango. The long summer evening, the music ... "Why do you treat me this way?" she asks. "I love you, of course ..." "I hate you," she says. He takes her hand and pulls her close. "Be careful ... my husband ... He has a pistol." He doesn't. She made that up. They are careful of the steps, the turns. It is complicated and they are intense, breathless ... the other dancers close by. But it is night that is important, the breeze is warm in the beckoning aspen grove where there are lovely grassy clearings. The stars are appearing one by one, and the moon is a mere beginning over the lake, a sliver in the indigo sky.

When the music ends he says, "Thank you, my dear." And she says, "Oh no, thank you!"

IN LESS THAN TEN MINUTES

You have to loosen a bolt that's stuck and does not want to budge, god knows why, it was torqued to specs with the finest tools. It is a very delicate operation, the bolt must not be broken. In order to do this you have to work standing on your head. And because of that your white tie drops down into your spaghetti sauce and you break a button that holds up your pants and in less than ten minutes the King of Bhutan is going to present you with an award. Well, you can tie up your pants with the cord that you wear around your neck that holds your ID card, which will then dangle between your legs, and you can paint your tie with more sauce so that it will appear that you have very bad taste, rather than being merely clumsy ... This is the kind of thing we like to do.

AMBITION

One of the good things about getting older is that no one asks anymore "What are you going to be when you grow up?" Or later on, "What do you do?" Questions for which I never had a good answer. Nowadays everyone assumes I'm retired, and that I have no ambition whatsoever. It isn't true. It is true that it's too late for me to become an Olympic champion swimmer or a lumberjack, but my ambitions are on higher things. I want to be a cloud. I'm taking some classes and have a really good instructor. I don't want to be a threatening storm cloud, just one of those sunny summer clouds. Not that I won't have a dark side, of course. I'd like to be one of those big fat cumulus clouds that pass silently overhead on a beautiful day. A day so fine, in fact, that you might not even notice me, as I sailed over your town on my way somewhere else, but you'd feel good about it.

THE WEDDING

"Where is the wedding? What time does it start?" "I don't know. What did you do with the invitation? What shall I wear?" Someone said it was at St. Paul's, then someone else said that at the last minute the couple decided to fly to Las Vegas and get married at a drive-up chapel. Never mind. It's the ideal wedding, the ideal couple.

Turns out we've missed the ceremony. As we arrive the minister is walking away from the church carrying his robes over his arm. It was hotter than usual today. He is smiling slightly as he walks, thinking of the newlyweds, thinking of a gin and tonic.

The old folks have gathered on the church lawn to chat. Summer hats, white shoes, pink dresses, powder blue sport coats. "Who was the bride?" No one is sure. The granddaughter of a friend? A distant cousin's niece? "But wasn't the bride beautiful?" "And the groom, so handsome—well, everyone says he's smart, has a very important job."

Meanwhile the bride and groom have gone to the rose garden to be photographed. Clouds are gathering in the west. Thunderstorms are predicted. It makes us unreasonably happy to see the bride and groom in their silly outfits, smiling at the camera—the air full of threat and promise, the smell of rain and of roses.

COLD NIGHT

Doors that once opened at a touch refuse to move, and machinery whose friendship you so casually assumed, won't work and is dangerous to touch barehanded. Everything that once seemed so alive is immobile and dumb, but something, long asleep, stirs. A yawn in the beams beneath the floor startles you. What is it? Outside, there is no wind. Smoke from the chimney makes ponderous and eerie shapes that move lightly along the ground by the window, and for a moment before it vanishes in the trees, the shape of someone safely forgotten. "It's no one," you think, to reassure yourself. "No one alive walking around on a night this cold."

MARCH

It hadn't occurred to me until someone at work brought it to my attention that this winter has been going on for eleven years. I said, "That can't be. Surely not." But then I got thinking about it. It was eleven years ago November we moved into this house. You remember, snow was just beginning and we had so much trouble getting the refrigerator down the driveway and through the door. Danny was eight and we got him a sled for Christmas. It's amazing how one gets concerned with other things and the time just goes by. Here it is March and now that I've noticed it, the snow has begun to melt a little. During the day there's water running in the street. It's like a bird singing in a tree that flies just as you become aware of it. When you think about it, the world, cold and hard as it is, begins to fall apart.

MARRIAGE

He said "People say marriage is like a three-legged race, but in our case she and I are tied together facing in the opposite directions on the stairs—she heading toward the main floor with the carpets and the furniture and such, and me heading to the basement with the furnace and the laundry tubs. It's okay, we get along, going nowhere, but it's damned difficult for the children or anyone else to get by us, whichever way they are headed."

RASPBERRY RHUBARB PIE

Ann has just taken one of her famous pies from the oven, and the crust has separated all around the perimeter so that the hot filling bubbles up, like lava from a Hawaiian volcano. It is very hot. The crust of the pie floats on the hot filling the way the earth's surface floats on its core of molten magma. Perhaps the center of the earth is hot raspberry-rhubarb filling, but you can't have any, it is much too hot. You are going to have to wait a very long time before you can have any.

MAILBOXES

Some are brightly painted and large as if anticipating great packages. Most are smaller, gray and dented with rust spots; some held together with rope or duct tape, having been slapped more than once by the snow plow. Still they seem hopeful ... perhaps a Village Shopper or a credit card offer ... Once in awhile one raises a modest tin flag. "I have something. It isn't much. I'd like you to take it." All along Highway 2, on Hunter Road and Dahl Road, past Cane Lake, past the gravel pit, and the last refrigerator shot full of holes and dumped into the swamp, mailboxes reach out on extended arms, all the way to the end of the route where balsam and spruce crowd together in the ditches, reaching out ...

A NEW POEM

I am driving again, the back roads of northern Minnesota, on my way from A to B, through the spruce and tamarack. To amuse myself I compose a poem. It is the same poem I wrote yesterday, the same poem I wrote last week, the same poem I always write, but it helps to pass the time. It's September and everything has gone to seed, the maple leaves are beginning to turn and the warblers are on their way south. The tansy and goldenrod in the ditches are covered with dust. Already my hair has turned gray. The dark comes much earlier now. Soon winter will come. I sigh and wonder, where has the time gone?

WHY?

I ask myself. Because when you finally need to go home this is the only place to go to. And when you get there there's nothing; just the blank page. Well, maybe there's a patch of dry bare ground, underneath an old cottonwood tree, a bit of sun, a crow in the next field. You can add things or take them away. Youth was the age of acquisition. Now you find that there aren't many things you need, but the garage and the attic are still full. I'm OK with the dirt and the cottonwood tree. It's not the bodhi tree, but my expectations are not high. The oceans are deep and dark and the briny water goes on for thousands of miles, but you only need a cupful or so to drown in.

THE PROSE POEM

The prose poem is not a real poem, of course. One of the major differences is that the prose poet is incapable, either too lazy or too stupid, of breaking the poem into lines. But all writing, even the prose poem, involves a certain amount of skill, just the way throwing a wad of paper, say, into a wastebasket at a distance of twenty feet, requires a certain skill, a skill that, though it may improve hand-eye coordination, does not lead necessarily to an ability to play basketball. Still, it takes practice and thus gives one a way to pass the time, chucking one paper after another at the basket, while the teacher drones on about the poetry of Tennyson.

YELLOW HAT

Nobody knows what will happen, what catastrophes, what miraculous transformations. In order to maintain faith, to plan for the future, the world must be simplified. Here is the window out of which you can see a tree, a bright red flower, green grass extending over the hill. On top of the hill, yes, there I am ... two legs, two arms, ten fingers like sausages and a smile on my big round face. And just six inches above my yellow hat the blue sky begins.

HIDDEN MEANINGS

Once I thought that things had meanings, that perhaps the river flowing, the wind moving a maple branch was a kind of secret signal being sent, a signal, a meaning that always just eluded me. It seemed that if I spread my arms that same wind could carry me into the sky. Now that I am old I happily realize that things and incidents, the bright red leaves tossing in the wind, beautiful as ever on the hillside, the secret world, has no meanings to impart, no hidden messages. But that, too, eludes me.

THINGS DON'T GO

Things don't go the way you want them to go. If you think the handle turns to the right, it turns to the left. Whichever way you think it turns, it turns the other way. It is no use trying to anticipate this; in every case it goes the other way. There's no use looking for your hat, it's on your head, where you will never see it. Whatever comes to you comes as a gift without your name on it. The moon wanders around the night sky, the sun rises, and a flock of birds lands briefly in the unmown grass.

WILL O' THE WISP

There are fewer birds now, an occasional group of fall warblers on their way south. The hummingbirds disappeared overnight. Patches of yellow here and there in the trees. It is the first day of fall, the season I once thought of as the most beautiful.

At night I stand by the window to try to spot one of those mysterious lights in the swamp down by the river, most often seen during the dark of the moon. Then they vanish. But all I see tonight is the dark reflection of myself in the glass.

LUCKY

All my life I've been lucky. Not that I made money, or had a beautiful house or cars. But lucky to have had good friends, a wife who loves me, and a good son. Lucky that war and famine or disease did not come to my doorstep. Lucky that all the wrong turns I made, even if they didn't turn out well, at least were not complete disasters. I still have some of my original teeth. All that could change, I know, in the wink of an eye. And what an eye it is, bright blue contrasting with her dark skin and black hair. And oh, what long eyelashes! She turns and with a slight smile gives me a long slow wink, a wink that says, "Come on over here, you lucky boy."

WHAT WE MEAN WHEN WE SAY
IT'S A BEAUTIFUL DAY

The summer was a disappointment, rain and cold wind. People say, "Last year summer was on a Tuesday, I think. I missed it because I had to work." The garden did not do well. Now it is fall, the leaves bright red, orange and gold in the sunshine, a beautiful day.

Someone says, "Isn't it a nice day?" "Beautiful!" is the proper response. That means the sun is shining, maybe only 32 degrees and the north wind a bit sharp, nevertheless we will not be pushed around. It is a beautiful day.

It means the wind has shifted. It means the snow has stopped falling. It means melt water is running in the street. It means we are still alive. It means the sun is shining and it is a beautiful day.

SHACK MADE OF STOLEN LINES

I lie long abed in the morning and listen to the barges on the Minnesota River. I lived for many years in the North, amongst the gloom of the tall pines and birches. It was beautiful, but too cold up there for an old man. But I may go back there one day. I know of a hunting shack I can use. It's not much, one room but it has a good cast-iron stove. It has been a late spring. Now mid-May, as I shuffle through the woods, hands in my pockets, a light snow begins to fall. It doesn't really matter, but I may ask myself, "Well, how did I get here?

NOTHING IN PARTICULAR

Head bowed, hands folded, I may look as if I am saying my prayers, and since I don't really believe in any religion you might say I am saying my prayers to nothing in particular. Or, to put a more positive spin on it, saying my prayers to everything in general, prayers to the chicken house, the freeway, the fading light and the dusty air. If you could see me sitting in my lawn chair on the back porch, it might appear that I have humbled myself before all the phenomena of the earth ... or that I have dozed off again in the late afternoon sun.

STORIES YOU TELL

There are worse things than being a human being, I suppose. You could be a politician, for instance. The only compensation for being human is that you can make up a good story. But good stories require a good audience, one that is patient and quiet. You could try telling a story to a cow. You'd want to gear the story to your audience. "Once upon a time I walked over by the fence and I stood there for a long time, chewing, looking out across the road ... then suddenly PLOP, I dropped a big cow pie. Ha ha ha ha!" The cow just stares at you, chewing. It's no good with dogs either, dogs listen, often with great enthusiasm, but they don't really get it. No good with cats or monkeys. That means you are pretty much stuck with other human beings as your audience. You spend a lifetime getting the stories just right and then you begin: "Once upon a time I walked over by the fence ..." and the listener stares into space, chewing, wondering vaguely how long this will last.

THOUGHTS GO THROUGH MY HEAD

Thoughts go through my head so swiftly but not as grand or important as lightning, more like static electricity, when your hair stands up for no reason, except dry air maybe, little tiny ideas, or the remnants of ideas, something like little blind kittens that will soon be drowned. The last thing I need, anyway, is more cats.

SMALL THINGS

Once you stood, brooding, on the cliff overlooking the turbulent sea and the tumultuous clouds, the wind blowing your long hair and the tails of your frock coat. Your role was to make as much noise as possible. Sturm und Drang. But what about the beautiful Marguerite? Ah, forget her ... the world so vast ...

Now your concerns have diminished somewhat. The seas continue to rise, the wind blows, the war goes on. You consider the wing of a bird, a stalk of grass, the late glimmer on the stream surface, realizing that this may be the last time you see any of these things again in this peculiar light. Small things. Like that sliver in the very tip of your finger that despite your best efforts resists removal, so small it is almost invisible, yet when you touch anything, it hurts.

SPRING WIND

The spring wind comes through and knocks over trash-cans and trees. It has something to do with warm fronts and cold fronts, I think, or with high and low pressure systems, things that I don't really understand and that aren't really an explanation anyway. Ultimately the spring wind is the result of some relationship between the earth and the sun that may not be all that healthy, after all. The wind comes in a big huff, slams doors, pushes things around and kicks up the dirt. The big bully spring wind comes through on its way nowhere and, ha ha! We love it.

THE AFTERLIFE

Older people are exiting this life as if it were a movie ... "I didn't get it," they are saying.

He says, "It didn't seem to have any plot."

"No." she says, "it seemed like things just kept coming at me. Most of the time I was confused ... and there was way too much sex and violence."

"Violence anyway," he says.

"It was not much for character development either; most of the time people were either shouting or mumbling. Then just when someone started to make sense and I got interested, they died. Then a whole lot of new characters came along and I couldn't tell who was who."

"The whole thing lacked subtlety."

"Some of the scenery was nice."

"Yes."

They walk on in silence for a while. It is a summer night and they walk slowly, stopping now and then, as if they had no particular place to go. They walk past a streetlamp where some insects are hurling themselves at the light, and then on down the block, fading into the darkness.

She says, "I was never happy with the way I looked."

"The lighting was bad and I was no good at dialogue," he says.

"I would have liked to have been a little taller," she says.

Louis Jenkins' poems have appeared in a number of literary magazines and anthologies. He has published ten collections of poetry. He was awarded two Bush Foundation Fellowships for poetry, a Loft-McKnight fellowship, and was the 2000 George Morrison Award winner. Mr. Jenkins has read his poetry on *A Prairie Home Companion* and was a featured poet at the Geraldine R. Dodge Poetry Festival in 1996 and at the Aldeburgh Poetry Festival, Aldeburgh, England in 2007.

Beginning in 2008, Louis Jenkins and Mark Rylance, Academy Award-winning actor and former director of the Globe Theatre, London, began work on a stage production titled *Nice Fish*, based on Mr. Jenkins poems. The play premiered April 6, 2013, at the Guthrie Theater in Minneapolis and ran through May 18, 2013. A revised version of the play was performed at American Repertory Theater in Boston (Jan-Feb 2016) where, thanks to Mark Rylance and Claire Van Kampen, Mr. Jenkins got a chance to attempt acting. It was a short-lived career. The play then moved to St. Ann's Warehouse in New York City (Feb-March 2016). In November 2016 the play opened at The Harold Pinter Theatre in London's West End, and ran until February 12, 2017. In March 2017 *Nice Fish* was nominated for an Olivier award as Best New Comedy of 2017.